THE GREAT DELUSION

A final wake up call to humanity

JASON CARTER

ISBN 9798873101610

THE
GREAT
DELUSION

A final wake up call to humanity

TRUMPET BLAST
PUBLISHING

Contents

TRUTH IS TREASON IN AN EMPIRE OF LIES

The Great Delusion

We are bombarded by distressing news whenever we switch the TV on — wars, viruses, climate change, and moral decay. The pervasive use of smartphones and social media has turned people into screen-focused zombies, even among lovers in restaurants fixated on individual screens.

Our culture is immersed in a fabricated reality—a world of edited selfies, deep fakes, virtual reality and artificial intelligence. Authenticity is scarce; the love of most grows cold, cynicism prevails, yet trust is reserved for mainstream media narratives.

The boundary between truth and falsehood blurs, grown men identify as little girls, 'men' give birth to 'theybie's', who are 'chestfed' by 'Maddy's'. Confused? More so, those promulgators of woke ideology. We live in a world of illusion, intoxicated by movies showcasing computer-generated heroes defying reality.

While we often associate propaganda with distant places like China or Russia, could we be unknowingly subjected to it in the West? What if our perceptions are being subtly shaped, steering us towards a predetermined narrative? What if the course of our world is orchestrated, not accidental?

Embark on a brief exploration about our current state of affairs in this concise book. *The Great Delusion: A final wake up call to humanity,* lays bare the contemporary war on Western culture, illuminating its current trajectory and providing guidance on how individuals can be rescued from surrendering body and soul to the rising world order.

Brace yourself for a paradigm-shifting exploration that challenges conventional perspectives on the world.

Navigating a Turbulent Global Landscape

As our world becomes further plunged into chaos, Islam and equally those siding with it will gain further prominence and power. This alliance will result in a social unrest never witnessed, rioting in our streets and a battle more overtly against who Islam call, 'the people of the book'. As Islamic culture finds acceptance in the West, the foundation upon which Western civilisation was built, becomes increasingly rejected.

UN Special Representative for International Migration, Peter Sutherland said, *"The EU should "do its best to undermine" the "homogeneity"* (cultural uniformity) *of its member states."*

Through the destabilisation of countries like Libya, Syria, Iraq and Afghanistan the globalists have unleashed a wave of migration into Europe, undermining the foundations of European culture.

Mass migration is fast-tracking the Islamization of the continent. Otherwise known as immigration jihad — a strategy of Islam.

Today Muslims migrate to Europe with the aim of

installing Sharia Law. Islamic scholar Abdessamad Belhaj said, *"Migration is seen as a beginning of the Islamization of Europe..."*

Pope Francis noted the European migration crisis to be an *"Arab Invasion"*. Undercover footage broadcast on Danish TV showed head imam of the Islamic Union in Denmark, Mohammad Fouad al-Barazi, admit that the goal of the migrant influx is for Muslims to conquer Europe. Sheikh Muhammed Ayed gave the order from the Al-Aqsa Mosque in Jerusalem that Muslims should use the migrant crisis to *"conquer their countries"*.

A Syrian refugee interviewed on Arabic television also spoke of his goal to "Islamize" Europe by converting its citizens. The UK has approximately 85 Sharia courts, run by clerics who support amputation for theft, marital rape, wife-beating, and child marriage.

The disintegration of civil society paves the way for a globalist vision aiming for a new era in human history. Those orchestrating behind the scenes seize every significant crisis. Rahm Emanuel, Chief of Staff to Obama admitted, *"You never let a serious crisis go to waste. And what I mean by that it's an opportunity to do things you think you could not do before."*

The intentional orchestration of frightening crises is one of the most successful means for inducing a change of mind within large numbers of people.

Crises, in short, are the means by which minds are controlled. Crises are being created by those with a globalist agenda.

Crises are the launchpad for world government agendas.

The Power of Crisis

We need to understand that a crisis is a powerful weapon in the hands of the globalists, and it is currently through crises that world government moves ever closer into actualisation.

To do that, the globalists are using a strategy known as the Hegelian Dialectic.

The Hegelian Dialectic creates a series of circumstances which guide our thoughts and actions towards a predetermined solution.

The Hegelian Dialectic derives its name from Georg Wilhelm Friedrich Hegel, a German philosopher (1770-1831). Hegel revolutionized European philosophy and was a forerunner to Marxism. Karl Marx used Hegel's dialectic theory to support his economic theory of communism and it was on this philosophical foundation that the ideology of the Soviet Union was built.

In simplistic terms the Hegelian Dialectic brings about change in three simple steps — **Problem, Reaction, Solution**.

For an example of this kind of cynical exploitation of peoples' minds through the use of fear-evoking crises let's look at COVID-19.

The **problem** was a *virus,* the **reaction** was *fear and panic,* the **solution** was *authoritarian surveillance and control.*

Existing AI surveillance cameras developed by Vivacity began registering distance between pedestrians, CCTV cameras were used to catch businesses open during lockdown, UK police used drones to catch dog walkers in remote areas, threats of shopping cart searches were made, as chief constable Nick Adderley, said his force was *"only a few days away"* from *"marshalling supermarkets and checking the items in baskets and trolleys to see whether it's a legitimate, necessary item."*

Moreover, vaccine certificates were distributed for numerous public venues, prohibiting entry to those who failed to comply. Mandatory PCR testing and quarantine measures were enforced, accompanied by the threat of fines for rule violations. The widespread adoption of phone monitoring, contact tracing apps, facial recognition technology, and automatic number-plate recognition (ANPR) was implemented to identify individuals suspected of breaching the UK lockdown.

Disturbingly, many of these surveillance measures persist beyond a crisis, enduring even after the threat has subsided. This results in a lasting state of heightened governmental control over the populace, surpassing the levels experienced prior to the crisis.

Under any other scenario the solution would have been flatly opposed by the people. But now, as a result of the crisis, the people cry out for the very solution they would have opposed which in turn is the solution that the globalists wanted and planned all along. The people now feel free from fear but are actually enslaved more than ever before to the government.

The Hegelian Dialectic is effective because it creates the illusion that the people are in control of their own destinies and that democracy is alive and well. It keeps the people in the dark as to what is truly going on. It also creates a certain dependency upon the government and the people look to it as though it is their only hope — when the exact opposite is true.

This is therefore the most effective deception.

For the globalist, the Hegelian cycle looks like this:

The Great Reset: Unveiling Its Significance and Impact

Klaus Schwab, founder of the World Economic Forum, said of the COVID-19 crisis, *"The pandemic represents a rare but narrow window of opportunity to reflect, reimagine, and reset our world."*

The push for a Great Reset was announced in 2014 by Klaus Schwab. Schwab said, *"What we want to do in Davos this year is to Push the Reset Button, the world is too much caught in a crisis mode."*

In 2016 Schwab was interviewed by RTS, the Swiss French language TV network, regarding implanting microchips into humans. He said, *"What we see is a kind of fusion of the physical, digital and biological world."*

Asked when this would happen, Schwab confidently stated, *"Certainly in the next ten years … We could imagine that we will implant them in our brain or in our skin … And then we can imagine that there is direct communication between the brain and the digital World."*

The COVID-19 response was not about controlling a virus. COVID-19 was the crisis launchpad to *'reimagine'* and *'reset our world.'*

COVID-19 and The Great Reset share an inseparable connection, as unveiled in Schwab's book *COVID-19: The Great Reset,* published during the Covid era. In this work, Schwab reveals a dystopian plan to fundamentally reshape society.

The Great Reset heralds a draconian overhaul encompassing economic, social, and governmental realms. Traditional notions of property ownership, such as homes and cars, will become obsolete. Instead, a new era will dawn, characterised by the prevalence of a digital currency and social credit scoring system. Fossil fuels will be banned, supplanted by a reliance on green energy sources.

Moreover, humanity will undergo a transformative upgrade through the integration of implants and genetic engineering, a procedure referred to as 'hacking humans' by proponents of The Great Reset. Sound like fantasy? It is anything but.

A Ministry of Defence document on the British government website confirms the reality, when it describes, *'Creating genetically modified humans'.* The document reads, *'Combining genetic engineering with artificial intelligence is likely to lead to radical improvements in medicine.'*

In a future projection the document claims that human augmentation (the technological and biological enhancement of the human body) was *'first accepted with great enthusiasm',* but these technologies *'were found to be unsafe or had side effects ... some of them serious.'*

The document predicts by 2045, *'the development of, what was in effect, a universal* **vaccine** *for all diseases. This led to global acceptance of human augmentation.'*

It is crucial to recognise that according to the British government document, vaccines are viewed as integral to human augmentation. Furthermore, the document acknowledges in its projection that the vaccines were deemed unsafe and carried significant side effects.

But is it a future reality or has experimentation begun now? During the COVID-19 vaccine rollout, Facebook's vaccine policy said they would remove any content that *'Claims that the COVID-19 vaccine changes people's DNA.'* But a leaked video from Facebook's CEO, Mark Zuckerberg had him claiming that very thing! Zuckerberg said, *"I share some caution on this because we just don't know the long-term side effects of basically modifying people's DNA and RNA."* This demonstrates two bombshells; one, the elite know the COVID-19 vaccine can change human DNA, and two, they are censoring that fact. They do not want the general public to know.

Individuals are experiencing gaslighting concerning The Great Reset. A simple Google search produces numerous pages dismissing the plan as a mere conspiracy theory. However, a visit to the World Economic Forum website unequivocally establishes its legitimacy and ongoing implementation. So too Schwab remains unfamiliar to most, as the media deliberately avoids drawing attention to him. Today, the problem lies in people's reluctance to engage in research, as they often prefer relying on mainstream media soundbite spin.

The WEF presents this reset as the Fourth Industrial Revolution. WEF say, *"The Fourth Industrial Revolution represents a fundamental change in the way we live, work and relate to one another. It is a new chapter in human development … These advances are merging the physical, digital and biological worlds in ways that create both huge promise and potential peril."*

Gone are the days of secrecy in globalist Bilderberg meetings or elite romps in the Redwood Forests of San Francisco at Bohemian Grove where leaders meet before a stone owl to perform occult rituals. In the present, globalists openly discuss their plan to transform the world, revealing their intentions to turn humans into cyborgs. Through this candid discourse, they normalise and condition the populace to accept a disconcerting vision prepared for them.

WEF Agenda Contributor Yuval Noah Harari unabashedly recounts the utilisation of COVID-19 to propel the digital age, surveillance, and achieve total control over the people. Harari said, *"…when people look back, the thing they will remember from the Covid crisis is, this is the moment when everything went digital, and this was the moment when everything became monitored, that we agreed to be surveyed all the time … Maybe most importantly of all, **this was the moment when surveillance started going under the skin** … the big process that's happening right now in the world is hacking human beings. The ability to hack humans, … Having the ability to really monitor people under the skin, this is the biggest game-changer of all. Because this is the key for getting to know people better than they know themselves … This is the crucial revolution and Covid is critical because this is what convinces people to accept, to legitimise total biometric surveillance."* (emphasis added)

What exactly did Harari mean when he stated the Covid crisis was the moment surveillance started going under the skin?

WEF's future is totalitarian, with self-determination becoming an ideal of the past. Harari stated, *"Humans are now hackable animals. The whole idea that humans have this soul or spirit, and they have freewill, and nobody knows what's happening inside me, so whatever I choose, whether in the elections, or whether in the supermarket, this is my freewill — that's over."*

Western civilisation must fall before this Great Reset can rise upon the world stage.

However, a Christian value system stands in the way of this global reset. According to Marxist philosopher and politician, Antonio Gramsci, the root of Christianity must be cut. Gramsci stated, *"...the civilized world has been thoroughly saturated with Christianity for 2000 years. Any country grounded in Judeo-Christian values cannot be overthrown until those roots are cut. But to cut the roots — to change culture — a long march through the institutions is necessary. Only then will power fall into our laps like a ripened fruit."*

Dictatorships face inherent challenges when contending with a society grounded in a belief system centred on God. The elimination of Christianity becomes imperative for the ascent of authoritarian rule, as the void left by the absence of divine allegiance paves the way for a transfer of loyalty to the ruling authorities. In this altered landscape, the people's gaze shifts away from a benevolent God, and the authorities emerge as de facto gods, wielding influence and control over the masses in the absence of a higher power.

We see this playing out in China and North Korea. It took place in the old Soviet Union and in Nazi Germany. To remove God from society, Jews, Christians, and other religious groups were eliminated. Germany adopted a Nazified form of Christianity that focused on worship of the state.

Are We Truly Free Thinkers?

The governing authority must institute a Ministry of Truth tasked with distorting both current and historical events, shaping public opinion through control of news media, entertainment, arts, and education.

This prompts us to ask: Are we genuine free thinkers, or have our opinions been deliberately sown?

The propagandist Edward Bernays answers this question. Bernays was hired by US presidents, and large corporations to spearhead and engage in propaganda campaigns.

Bernays wrote: *'If we understand the mechanism and motives of the group mind, is it not possible to control and regiment the masses according to our will without their knowing about it?'*

And again, *'In almost every act of our daily lives, whether in the sphere of politics or business, in our social conduct or our ethical thinking, we are dominated by the relatively small number of persons who understand the mental processes and social patterns of the masses. It is they who pull the wires which control the public mind.'*

According to Bernays the true ruling power belongs to an invisible government, not what we see showcased via the mainstream media. This unseen group is made up of those who control the masses through complex propaganda techniques and deceive the people into believing that their ideas are their own, when they have been strategically implanted.

The state restricts news from unauthorised sources, employing surveillance and censorship as crucial instruments to stifle both free speech and critical thinking.

Mass Media, Mass Manipulation

In 1969 scientist Herbert Krugman found that in less than a minute watching television, brain waves move from *Beta* waves — active logical thought — to *Alpha* waves that are meditative and open to suggestion, as in hypnosis. Television is therefore an effective means for deceiving the masses through the transmission of propaganda.

Television has created a false reality that encourages dependency and subjects the masses to continuous daily manipulation and lies.

Project Mockingbird was a Central Intelligence Agency (CIA) secret project in the late 1940s.

The operation was to recruit and put on the CIA payroll American news agencies and journalists to buy influence behind the scenes at the major media outlets and to become distributors of government propaganda.

William Colby, former CIA Director said, *'the CIA owns everyone of any significance in the major media.'*

The status quo persists, as this strategy continues to be employed at our expense, minute by minute.

During the Covid era, trust in the system surged throughout the Western world.

Ask yourself, when were politicians believed, or when was Big Pharma ever trusted? But society not only trusted, but they also set a terrifying precedent. They offered up their bodies to them.

Society fell under a spell. Our world became bewitched, as mankind sacrificed itself upon the altar of government, and the march toward global tyranny advanced.

Pre-Covid, many felt empowered, a return to individual freedom filled the air. A healthy pride in national identities was gaining momentum across the world. Could democracy actually be functioning? Many began to wonder. But the globalists were not going to idly sit back and do nothing. To regain lost ground a serious crisis was required.

Amid the deliberately lacklustre BBC and SkyNews Brexit coverage on January 31, 2020, Covid propaganda was tactically woven into the narrative. A massive distraction was underway. News flashes of the China virus drama supplanted a pivotal moment in British politics. Fears of a looming global health scare overshadowed Britain's departure from the European Union. Was this a mere coincidence?

Across the pond, so too a calculated response was required.

In 2017 Doctor Anthony Fauci, director of the National Institute of Allergy and Infectious Diseases, said, *"There is no question that there will be a challenge to the coming administration in the arena of infectious diseases … also there will be a surprise outbreak."*

No question? A surprise outbreak? How could Fauci have been so confident?

Ron Johnson, member of Senate Homeland Security suggested the pandemic was pre-planned by an *"elite group of people"*. Johnson cited Event 201, a pandemic exercise conducted October 2019 as evidence.

Johnson said, *"This is all pre planned by an elite group of people … Event 201 that occurred in late 2019, prior to the rest of us knowing about this pandemic. Again, this is very concerning in terms of what has happened, what is happening, what continues to be planned for our loss of freedom."*

Johnson added, *"It needs to be exposed. But unfortunately, there are very few people, even in Congress that are willing to take a look at this. They all push the vaccine. They don't want to be made aware of the fact that the vaccines might have caused injuries, might have caused death. So many people just simply don't want to admit they were wrong, and they're going to do everything they can to make sure that they're not proven wrong."*

Event 201 simulated a global pandemic of a coronavirus transmitted by bats. The simulation was an exact prediction of the COVID-19 pandemic declared just 20 weeks later. The event, in October 2019, was hosted by Johns Hopkins Center for Health Security, the World Economic Forum, and the Bill and Melinda Gates Foundation. Event 201 resulted in an agreement among representatives from various societal sectors to craft a narrative. This narrative was intended for use by both governmental entities and the mainstream media, with the aim of embedding it within the global population. They deliberated on strategies to address so called misinformation disrupting the pandemic response, exploring options such as deleting Facebook and Twitter accounts disseminating 'false' information. In a simulated news report, it was stated, *"If the solution means controlling and reducing access to information, I think it's the right choice."*

Was Event 201 merely a coincidence? In 2010 the Rockefeller Foundation imagined a future pandemic, eerily similar to the COVID-19 pandemic. In the document, *'Scenarios for the Future of Technology and International Development,'* it describes how a virus was used to bring in a biometric ID for all citizens and how an authoritarian government was willingly accepted by the people in return for their health and safety.

It outlined the enforcement of mandatory face masks, implementation of body temperature checks at entrances to train stations and supermarkets, and the cessation of travel, tourism, supply chains, as well as the closure of shops and offices. The document praised China for its pandemic response, exactly as occurred during the COVID-19 pandemic.

The opening paragraph under *Lock Step* reads, *'In 2012, the pandemic that the world had been anticipating for years finally hit.'*

The document states, *'Citizens willingly gave up some of their sovereignty—and their privacy—to more paternalistic states in exchange for greater safety and stability. Citizens were more tolerant, and even eager, for top-down direction and oversight, and national leaders had more latitude to impose order in the ways they saw fit. In developed countries, this heightened oversight took many forms: biometric IDs for all citizens, for example...'*

These are carefully crafted plans, masquerading as simulations and scenarios. COVID-19 was not a random event; rather, it represented the culmination of extensive time and preparation leading up to it. Everything was in place before they pressed play on 2020.

Understanding this helps to foretell possible future crisis events in the pipeline and to prepare accordingly.

According to WEF, Great Reset architect, Klaus Schwab, a *"cyber pandemic"* is coming. Schwab describes the event; *"The frightening scenario of a comprehensive cyber attack which would bring to a complete halt to the power supply, transportation, hospital services, our society as a whole.* ***The COVID-19 crisis would be seen in this respect as a small disturbance*** *in comparison to a major cyber attack."* (emphasis added)

Jeremy Jurgens, WEF Managing Director said, *"I believe that there will be another crisis.* ***It will be more significant. It will be faster than what we've seen with Covid.*** *The impact will be greater, and as a result the economic and social implications will be even more significant."* (emphasis added)

The Cyber Polygon 2021 event was conducted by the Prime Minister of the Russian Federation Mikhail Mishustin together with Klaus Schwab of the World Economic Forum.

"A cyber attack with COVID-like characteristics would spread faster and farther than any biological virus," comments the WEF.

An effective cyber attack could compromise any system connected to the internet, including; life saving medical devices, the internet, personal bank accounts and global financial systems, energy grids, water treatment facilities, government systems and military infrastructure.

The reconstruction of nations in the aftermath of a

sweeping cyber attack could demand a complete societal overhaul, aligning precisely with the objectives of the Great Reset. This could also include a purging of the internet, resulting in the permanent loss of independent journalism, current and historical fact, and all dissenting voices.

Will Klaus Schwab's *'cyber pandemic'* actually occur in the following years, or is the WEF using the possibility to further advance the Great Reset agenda? Either way, it will play right into their hands.

Through trauma-based mind control, employing one crisis after the other, the hypnotised masses are faced with a barrage of apocalyptic scenarios. Be it virus, war, terrorism, climate change, cyber attack — you name it, but always, the world will end, unless this unelected behemoth steps in to save the planet.

How the 'Save Lives' Mantra Influenced the Masses

'Save lives' the oft repeated mantra during Covid, conditioned the masses to trust unequivocally in their benevolent guardians. These protectors then arm to the teeth any nation they can exploit in their quest, even if it means risking nuclear conflict in their pursuit of world revolution.

These 'life savers' advocate for depopulation, arguing that earth is facing challenges due to high population numbers.

Both artificial intelligence and robotics assist in the plan of depopulation as humans become obsolete in the new order. By 2025 China will mass-produce humanoid robots that can perform various tasks and interact with humans. Under the guise of convenience people are becoming dispensable. As high street banks close, unstaffed and cashless shops spring up in preparation for a world with less people.

Meanwhile people will be herded into planned 15-minute cities, where services, shopping, education, healthcare, and entertainment can be easily reached by a 15-minute walk, bike ride, or public transport from any point in the city eliminating the need for cars.

Saudi Arabia's, The Line, a trillion-dollar smart city slicing through the Tabuk desert, is a world without cars. A train running from end to end, volocopters, delivery drones and robot servants, The Line is the ultimate manifestation of the dystopian nightmare organised for humanity's future.

Sound like science fiction? It's far from it. Work began on the smart city in October 2021, with residents planned to move in during 2024. The first phase of the project will be completed by 2030, dovetailing perfectly with the United Nations 2030 Agenda.

The 2030 Agenda is yet another strategy toward global government. One stated goal is to end poverty everywhere. In other words, to put everyone on government welfare, consistent with the World Economic Forum's prediction that by 2030, *"You'll own nothing and be happy."*

After 2035 it will be illegal to sell a petrol or diesel car in the European Union, while short-haul flights are being banned now. Truth is, the elite do not want the masses to travel. They want them to stay in their own backyard, not for lofty reasons of cutting CO2 and valiantly saving the planet, but for ease of monitoring and controlling the populace.

Former Prime Minister, Boris Johnson wrote a piece for the Telegraph entitled *Global over-population is the real issue,* in which he stated, *'The primary challenge facing our species is the reproduction of our species itself.'*

While advisor to Klaus Schwab, Yuval Noah Harari openly stated the elites contempt for mankind, *"This perhaps* *is going to be the biggest question in 21st century economics and politics — **What to do with billions of useless humans.***" (emphasis added)

Furthermore, in a TED Talks presentation in 2010, Bill Gates mused, *"First we've got population. The world today has 6.8 billion people. That's headed up to about 9 billion. Now if we do a really great job on new vaccines, healthcare, reproductive healthcare services, we could lower that by perhaps 10 or 15 percent."*

Save lives? Only the hypnotised masses could believe such blatant lies and hypocrisy.

But the British public was continually exposed to the daily 'save lives' message, subtly conditioning and propagandising them to believe the opposite of the reality unfolding behind closed doors.

But so few are able, or willing to join the dots — the man who advocates to depopulate the world also runs an international vaccine industry. In 2010, the Gates Foundation funded experimental malaria and meningitis vaccine trials across Africa and HPV vaccine programs in India. All these programs resulted in many deaths and injuries, with accounts of forced vaccinations and uninformed consent.

Disguised as philanthropists, one can literally get away with murder.

Gates YouTube channel was a dead giveaway. Throughout lockdown, all user comments on most videos alluded to, or outright spoke of a depopulation agenda. Initially, comments were disabled, but as users expressed dissent through thumbs down votes, YouTube eventually removed this feature to obscure public opinion.

Gates intents are denied by the masses. Slurs of 'conspiracy theorist' are employed by those unwilling to believe that a widely recognised figure, donning a cheerful pink sweater, could hint at anything remotely sinister.

This brings to mind a statement made by J Edgar Hoover, FBI director, *"The individual is handicapped by coming face to face with a conspiracy so monstrous they cannot believe it exists."*

In psychology, this phenomenon is termed cognitive dissonance. When individuals encounter unsettling truths conflicting with their worldview, instead of contemplating the information, they promptly dismiss it in favour of a more idealised perspective.

Who Fact-checks the Fact-checkers?

To substantiate the evidence that something nefarious is afoot, don't bother Googling it. You'll get the fact-checker spin. But ask yourself, who fact-checks the fact-checkers?

Thanks to a lawsuit that exposed the war on so-called misinformation, Facebook admitted their fact-checking to be nothing more than opinion. They are merely politically motivated, points of view, not facts.

Upon uncovering that a Facebook fact-checker discrediting reports that COVID-19 leaked from a lab in Wuhan was employed at the same lab, further raises doubts about the credibility of their 'facts.'

Furthermore, the reliability of Snopes, the well-known fact-checking website, came into question after its founder faced allegations of fraud, deceit, and questionable expenses involving prostitutes.

When confronted with an irrefutable report, many fact-checkers deceptively highlight minor factual errors. While insignificant to the story's overall validity, divert the reader's attention.

The fact-checking industry is financially supported by the likes of George Soros, government-funded non-profit organisations, Big Pharma and tech giants. This backing raises questions about the impartiality of fact-checkers as unbiased arbiters of truth.

China: The Rising Force as a Global Superpower

When triumphant a global dictatorship will finally replace any last vestige of individual nationhood and biblical roots.

As a model, think China. This is a soon coming reality. China is the globalist blueprint. Finally, the puppeteers are ready to make their move with China onto the world stage.

The future is cashless, accelerated during COVID-19, and transitioning towards digital currencies. COVID-19 played a pivotal role in the rise of the QR code. Rolled out everywhere from scanning a restaurant menu to not least on vaccine passports. Unless a person had the 'mark', they were forbidden from entering public spaces or in making a purchase.

Former World Bank analyst, Peter Koenig describes the QR code as, *"an all-electronic ID — linking everything to everything of each individual (records of health, banking, personal and private, etc.)."*

Furthermore, Elon Musk plans to revolutionise X into a financial hub by late 2024, in which Musk claims, *"you won't need a bank account."*

Accompanied also by the implementation of a social credit system based on the China model. The system will entail the curtailment of certain rights for noncompliance. In China, citizens face consequences such as restricted travel as a form of punishment.

In Beijing, October 2023, Xi Jinping, along with President Putin and notably United Nations Secretary General Antonio Guterres, *'hailed China as the only country capable of navigating the challenges of the 21st century.'*

The conditioning for the acceptance of the China model of rule gained momentum during the Covid lockdown, a fertile ground for propaganda to quickly take root. The stay home orders served to manipulate the masses on a global scale never seen in history. So also, lockdown functioned to segregate people, preventing them from discussing what could be going on.

With little else to do, a fear ridden, and demoralised people stared hopeless at their screens, and in their vulnerability fell ever deeper into the controller's hypnotic endgame.

Nothing is new. In the ruins of Berlin 1945 the Allies discovered plans for a cable television network. Hitlers minister for Public Enlightenment and Propaganda, Joseph Goebbels, the brainchild behind the project, said: *'we'll be able to show whatever we want. We'll create a reality, which the people of Germany need and can copy.'* Goebbels further stated, *'propaganda means repetition and still more repetition!'*

Same old same old. Repeatedly, the global population were subjected to a strategy of fear and manipulation. Emotionally blackmailed into submission, they obeyed nonsensical directives without question.

During Covid, behavioural scientists advising the UK government recommended that the people must be frightened. For the purpose of increasing adherence to social distancing the group said, *'a substantial number of people still do not feel sufficiently personally threatened,'* and, *'the perceived level of personal threat needs to be increased among those who are complacent, using hard-hitting emotional messaging'.*

Through manipulative marketing campaigns, a rolling death count displayed on TV screens in every home across the world, a reality was created, and the people succumbed to the most elaborate scam ever foisted upon humanity.

During lockdown, numerous concerned citizens, sensing that something was amiss, decided to pay a visit to their local hospitals, only to find them eerily deserted. The online circulation of several videos brought to light that this phenomenon was not an isolated occurrence. A news broadcast depicted long queues of people waiting for PCR tests, but a vigilant local captured the scene revealing an emptiness, with the broadcast crew instructing passersby to form a line solely for the camera.

In another revelation behind the scenes, a news broadcast covering a supposedly bustling pandemic ward exposed staged scenes of moving body bags and fake patients.

A whistleblower using the pseudonym Dr. John, who worked throughout the pandemic, disclosed that hospitals were unusually quiet and nearly vacant in the initial months of the April 2020 lockdown. Dr. John remarked, *"I used to attend to an average of 20 patients per day, and that dwindled to just 1-2 patients during the first lockdown."*

Adding to the disturbing findings, nurses, who

seemingly worked tirelessly to save lives, found time to perform offensive dance routines, exemplified by a TikTok video where a group of nurses danced with a fake body labelled 'Covid' affixed to its foot.

In an effort to artificially inflate statistics, fatalities were erroneously attributed to COVID-19, even when the cause of death was unrelated. For instance, a man involved in a fatal motorcycle crash in Florida was recorded as a COVID-19 casualty, despite health officials being aware of the actual circumstances surrounding his demise.

A Twitter user, identifying as a former National Health Service professional, highlighted the concerning practice of categorising various deaths, including those from pneumonia and other health conditions, as COVID-19-related. Patients with common ailments such as old age, myocardial infarctions, kidney failure, haemorrhages, strokes, Chronic Obstructive Pulmonary Disease, and cancer were all being classified as COVID-19 deaths upon admission and subsequent demise.

Adding to the controversy, Dr. John accused the government and NHS directors of instructing healthcare staff to let patients die, and in some instances deliberately kill them through the 'End of Life Care' program and falsely label the deaths as COVID-19.

Independent undertaker John O'Looney was contacted during COVID-19 by a government sponsored individual to gather data from all the funeral directors. O'Looney said, *"It wasn't too long before I felt that he was steering me, for an example, the conversation would go —*

[Government sponsored individual], *"Who have you collected this week?"*

"I've collected a gentleman from a care home, in his

nineties, there was no doctor present, no Covid test present, he wasn't Covid."

[Government sponsored individual] *"Oh but there was Covid in the care home, so he must have been."*

O'Looney continued, *"I collected a cancer patient from a hospice, he was terminally ill with cancer."*

[Government sponsored individual], *"Oh but he must have had Covid, because I've heard there was Covid in there."*

O'Looney said, *"Everyone, consistently was being labelled with Covid, and it was ridiculous. It was laughable. Even one guy that was run over was a Covid death…it didn't add up and alarm bells started ringing because they were making an unnatural effort to label everyone as a Covid death and I hasten to add, that the death rate actually wasn't any more, in fact it was a bit quieter than 2019."*

Such was the impact of fear-driven propaganda that even today, some are reluctant to step outside their homes. Others can be seen donning a proven ineffective, and bacteria infested mask. Or in queuing for a vaccine that failed to stop transmission as pledged but has rather taken the lives of untold millions in possibly the greatest censorship campaign in history.

COVID-19: Lies, Deception, and Hypocrisy

Meanwhile Prime Minister Boris Johnson, Rishi Sunak and other members of the British government revealed just how innocuous the virus truly was by blatantly partying together during lockdown, knowing there to be no real danger. A video surfaced from the gathering, of Downing Street Press Secretary, Allegra Stratton performing a mock press conference in which she joked about a party having taken place.

According to experts the virus not only has a 99% recovery rate, but inexpensive drugs like Hydroxychloroquine and Ivermectin were effective treatments for COVID-19. But try Googling, 'Ivermectin'.

In an effort to push Big Pharma's jab, over any other tried and tested treatment, the truth won't be found. On the contrary, an FDA warning is revealed online, *'Why You Should Not Use Ivermectin to Treat or Prevent COVID-19'*. In bed with the establishment, Google suppress anything that goes against the official narrative. Both drugs were made illegal or unavailable in order to justify *'emergency use authorisation'* of a costly 'vaccine' based on a technology, untested in humans, and rushed into production.

In 2014 the book *Trumpet Blast Warning* alerted —

*"...the nations will be duped in a massive deception both through the **media** and **pharmaceutical drugs**..."*

With chilling accuracy, the peoples of the earth were never more deceived by Big Pharma and their mainstream media cohort's. With lucrative contracts amassing billions, is it any wonder that together, along with big government and the mainstream media, truth is silenced?

Pfizer Confessions

An undercover journalist armed with hidden camera had Pfizer, Senior Associate scientist Chris Croce confess, *"I still feel like I work for an evil corporation because it comes down to profits in the end...Basically, our organization is run on Covid money now."* Croce continued, *"...you have multiple companies that were basically given a cr*p ton of money to produce vaccines and they're pushing them."*

But far more concerning is that according to Croce, Pfizer conducted tests to see if their vaccines were leading to heart attacks. The journalist said, *"I'm glad you didn't get any myocarditis. Cause that's a concern, right?"* Croce replied, *"Yeah. More so for younger people."* Why, asked the journalist. Croce responded, *"That's what we're looking into right now...we just sent, like, 3,000 patients' samples to get tested for like elevated troponin levels* (levels to detect heart attack) *to see if it's vaccine based...We'll see, hopefully it's good...if not then, my opinion, that might pull something from the market."*

To date the Pfizer jab has not recalled.

We can be thankful that true journalism exposing corruption is still alive, unlike at the BBC and CNN who speak only for the establishment.

But every now and again truth slips out. The BBC was taken off guard when cardiologist, Dr Aseem Malhotra, used his appearance to call for a suspension of the mRNA COVID-19 vaccine. Malhotra said, *"My own research has found...is that the **Covid mRNA vaccines do carry a cardiovascular risk.** And I've actually called for the suspension of this pending an enquiry, because there's a lot of uncertainty at the moment about what's causing the excess deaths."* (emphasis added)

Since the vaccine rollout, there has been a concerning surge in heart-related issues, notably cardiac arrests, leading to numerous athletes collapsing during games. While the official stance remains 'no correlation,' the post-vaccine era has prompted a widespread effort to deploy thousands of defibrillators in schools, public transport, and parks nationwide.

A press release on the British government website dated July 2023 headlines — *'Millions of children get access to life-saving defibrillators'.* The government ensured every state school in England has a defibrillator with 20,376 devices delivered to 17,862 schools.

In October 2023 the Mayor of London, Sadiq Khan, announced all London Underground and Overground stations now have public defibrillators, for the first time ever. Moreover, a £1 million fund was given for defibrillators in parks, post offices and shops to help those suffering cardiac arrest.

According to the British Heart Foundation, nearly

100,000 more people with cardiovascular disease than expected have died since the start of the pandemic in England. The Foundation said, this means that, on average, there have been over 500 additional deaths a week involving cardiovascular disease, since the pandemic began. They put it down to ongoing disruption to NHS heart care, and Covid-19, but fail to include the subsequent introduction of the Covid-19 vaccine on December 8, 2020 as possibly playing a part.

In deliberate omissions, news stories abound since the vaccine rollout of every other reason for a heart attack, including cold weather, *'Heart attack risk 'doubles' in cold weather warns doctor'*, reported the Daily Record. But hot weather too, *'Risk of fatal heart attack may double in heat wave'* read another story. Since the vaccine rollout, all kinds of normal activities can instantly kill healthy people. Now cold showers are lethal and video games too. Also be careful to get enough shut eye, as lack of sleep is leading to massive heart attacks!

Doomed to Repeat History

If only the masses understood history, they would know that a 1976 Swine Flu pandemic was used to initiate a frenetic vaccination programme. It ended in killing and paralysing perfectly healthy Americans in its wake. Incidentally the so-called pandemic totalled four cases and resulted in one fatality. Or if they briefly studied the Swine Flu pandemic scandal of 2009 maybe they would begin to open their eyes. The World Health Organisation projected up to 7.4 million could die. It did not happen.

The WHO declared influenza pandemic is now a documented hoax and the Council of Europe agreed they caused an international panic and disaster by declaring the **'mildest flu ever'**. WHO worked in tandem with Big Pharma to terrorise a trusting public. They rolled out a dangerous vaccination programme that harmed the lives of thousands, leaving them with serious and chronic health disorders.

Since the inception of COVID-19, propaganda accelerated to absurd levels. If it had not been for the relentless deluge of fear driven news and horrifying images disseminated through television, the pandemic would have otherwise been invisible.

The people were subjected to daily briefings reporting the number of deaths and hospitalisations that terrified people into staying at home. But from January 2023 excess deaths in the UK were higher than at the height of COVID-19, yet this received no airtime. From April to August 2022 there were 22,500 more deaths than expected in the UK. This surge was apparently unexplained. Why the media silence now? Why the absence of the Chief Medical Officer from our TV screens? What are they hiding? The silence is deafening.

Media Coercion of the Public

The public were bombarded minute-by-minute with vaccine propaganda. Celebrities, politicians, religious figures, and royalty used their influence to coerce the public.

Pope Francis who met secretly with Pfizer CEO on a few occasions and also with Melinda Gates called the vaccination *"a moral obligation."*

His UK counterpart, the Archbishop of Canterbury, Justin Welby was asked by ITV News at Ten if being vaccinated was a *"moral issue",* Welby responded, *"…Yes, I think it is."* The archbishop even implied that Jesus would get vaccinated. As did Franklin Graham, son of well-known US evangelist, the late Billy Graham. Upon being asked Graham said, *"Jesus Christ would advocate for people using vaccines."* While Queen Elizabeth II unusually weighed in, telling her subjects not to be selfish.

Never before was taking a pharmaceutical elevated to an act of religious piety. The procedure became more akin to an initiation ceremony into a global religious health cult, where those who desired not to be vaccinated were shunned as selfish, immoral sinners destined for hell.

In line with typical religious practices, the NHS in Britain, often dubbed the 'national religion', saw its followers encouraged by the mainstream media to gather weekly in the streets for worship. Those who declined to bow before the NHS logo or partake in the weekly clapping ritual found themselves facing disapproval from family and friends.

U.K. Prime Minister Boris Johnson, New Zealand's, Jacinda Ardern and Canada's, Justin Trudeau, U.S. President Joe Biden, singers Mariah Carey, Elton John, actors Arnold Schwarzenegger and Michael Cane — the list is endless, of all those who were enlisted to do their part to bolster the narrative that drove a wedge in society that destroyed families and friendships forever.

Those refusing the shot were denigrated at every turn. In Italy Vincenzo De Luca, President of Campania region, announced he would like to 'flamethrower the unvaccinated' and Tony Blair called those who refused the vaccine 'idiots'. Piers Morgan branded so called anti-vaxxers 'selfish pr*cks' after suggesting they should be 'thrown in a cave'. A two-tier society was created by instilling fear into the populace.

'Anti-vaxxer', 'conspiracy theorist', 'tin foil hat wearer', 'maskholes', 'covidiots' and 'granny killers', to name but a few derogatory terms banded about by the mainstream media were used to bully, discredit and silence anyone detailing facts, knowledge and insights that exposed corruption and evil.

Scientists Face Cancellation for Speaking Truth

Even notable scientists, virologists and experts in their field who attempted to tell a different story were cancelled, silenced, and ridiculed.

Michael Yeadon, ex-Pfizer chief scientist and vice-president of allergy and respiratory research who was vocal about the virus, masks, lockdowns, and the vaccine said, *"There never was a viral pandemic of a novel pathogen. I don't believe there has been a novel cause of significant illness and death, other than our government's responses to the fake 'pandemic,'"* he said. *"The deaths that we saw, I'm afraid, were medical malpractice at best and murder at worst. Basically, we were lied to from the beginning."*

From PCR tests to masks, to 'asymptomatic spread' is false, Yeadon warned. PCR tests, he said, *"don't tell you anything,"* and cloth masks, *"if anything make you more likely to catch an unusual bacterial pneumonia because you're breathing through a filthy cloth."*

Yeadon said, *"These vaccines that we know have harmed*

people, were they toxic by accident, or as I put it, toxic by design? Now I've spent thirty-two years in bio pharma research, I was a VP in Pfizer, head of worldwide research for respiratory, ten years in biotech I ran my own biotech that was sold to Novartis which was then the biggest drug company in the world. So, I'm not stupid. I know what I'm doing. … So, when I looked at the design of these so called vaccines, I found at least three things that I can describe quickly to you, that if you accept what I tell you, you can no longer believe that these are toxic accidentally. That is, they were designed to injure, to maim, and to kill …

So, the three items you should look at, when you're trying to make a vaccine like this, you have to choose which bit of the alleged pathogen you're going to pick to put into your vaccine. Now I would suggest to you, you pick a bit that was different from you and was not harmful. So, you might pic a bit of the virus that doesn't seem to do anything to you…. which bits did they pick? The spike protein, the bit on the outside, that's the bit that actually was known beforehand to be biologically really violently active, stimulating blood clotting, neurological problems and other things. All four drug companies picked spike protein. So, there you go, straight away I knew this was not an accident. Somebody was trying to harm people."

Dr Robert Malone, an mRNA inventor, (the technology used in the injection) warned, 'something has gone badly wrong.' Both Malone and Yeadon are now belittled on Wikipedia as peddling conspiracy theories.

Michael Yeadon speaking on COVID-19 said, *"You've been subject to propaganda and lies by people who are very well trained in how they do that."*

Meanwhile Andrew Bridgen MP, criticised the COVID-19 vaccines. Bridgen quoted an Israeli doctor when he tweeted the vaccines were, *"the biggest crime against humanity since the Holocaust."* Bridgen was expelled from the Conservative party for antisemitism.

Jewish scientists from around the world called on Prime Minister Rishi Sunak to withdraw the claim that Bridgen was guilty of making antisemitic comments. The letter stated, *"It seems that you and others have seized upon the opportunity to raise the issue of antisemitism in order to limit the free speech of those who raise legitimate concerns about the efficacy and safety of these Covid vaccines."*

In a parliamentary speech *Trends in Excess Deaths*, Bridgen said, *"the experimental COVID-19 vaccines are not safe and are not effective,"* and, *"It is high time that these experimental vaccines were suspended and a full investigation into the harms that they have caused was initiated."*

Furthermore, a groundbreaking study by Drs. Denis Rancourt, Marine Baudin, Joseph Hickey and Jérémie Mercier, discovered that to date 17 million people died worldwide after receiving the COVID-19 vaccine.

This should be garnering international attention and a call for an immediate cessation of all COVID-19 vaccines. Instead the shocking findings have been censored and 'fact-checked'. In the months and years to follow that disturbing figure is only set to rise.

Whistle blower politicians and experts in their field are lost in a sea of disinformation, censored and 'fact-checked' at every turn. Bridgen himself stated, *"There will be a full press pack going out to all media outlets following my speech, with all the evidence to back up all the claims I will make, but I do not doubt that there will be no mention of it in the mainstream media."*

Experts were mocked by comedians, turned cringeworthy specimens of a system hellbent on a global marketing campaign to get vaccinated.

A skit on Stephen Colbert's, *The Late Show* in the US, called *The Vax-Scene*, in which a dance troupe featuring performers dressed as syringes is possibly the most disturbing scene in show business.

As Colbert and his dancers jig up the isles to a hypnotic ditty inanely calling out 'vaccine', a mind-numbed audience clap along in robotic unison.

An article about a triple-jabbed man who apparently died from Covid claimed, if the victim had been unvaccinated, it would have been a lot worse. What could be worse than dying? Was it satire? No! It was a genuine story and perfectly illustrates the power of fear-based propaganda. Anything is believable if it is repeated often enough.

"By skilful and sustained use of propaganda, one can make a people see heaven as hell, or a most wretched life as paradise," said Adolf Hitler.

Conditioned for Authoritarianism

During lockdown the masses were conditioned to accept a new form of governance — one repressive and authoritarian.

Bill Gates praised China for its pandemic response, which others said could only have been achieved through its authoritarian form of government.

Chinese citizens were imprisoned and left to starve in their homes as law enforcement welded their doors shut. An elderly woman in the street, cruelly caged like an animal, could be seen peering confused through a tiny window. It was China who performed an anal PCR swab drive-through in broad daylight. Dehumanising techniques such as these break the human spirit and make subservient to the state.

China, well known for its human rights abuses, obviously did not bat an eyelid at these brutalising and downright sinister excuses for containment.

In an article for Xinhua News Bill Gates cites China as crucial for global health. Gates said, *"In the future, I expect China to play a critical role in global pandemic preparedness efforts."*

Bill Gates is the second largest donor to the World Health Organisation holding great sway over the organisation. Director-General Tedros Adhanom Ghebreyesus, leading the WHO, should face disqualification from any international office due to allegations of terrorism and human rights abuses during his tenure in the Ethiopian government from 2005 to 2016. The appointment of a human rights violator as the international head of global health highlights the WHO's questionable ethical foundations. These concerns are well-documented, not mere conspiracy theories.

WHO has proposed a global pandemic preparedness treaty urging all member states to sign. Once ratified, this treaty will override national governments, enabling WHO to call a health crisis in any nation. WHO's sweeping powers will give them authority to lockdown and vaccinate at will.

It is not difficult to see where this is heading.

Bill Gates has confidently declared there will be another pandemic.

The world awaits.

World Government Foretold Decades Ago

Under the guise of crisis treaties global governance is being accomplished. Over decades it has methodically developed, and now, in our era, we observe the execution of its final stages.

For instance, the United Nations Paris Climate Agreement is being used around the world to take control of earth's resources, while micromanaging human activity. According to those pushing the agenda, if humans eat insects, the weather will change. Simultaneously lab-grown and 3D printed meat will become the preferred norm, while of course the global elite tuck into a good old-fashioned steak.

Over seventy years ago it was under discussion. In 1950 James Warburg, financial advisor to U.S. President Roosevelt boldly proclaimed, *"We shall have world government whether or not you like it, by conquest or consent."*

So too Henry Kissinger, Secretary of State to President Nixon brazenly declared, *"Today America would be outraged if UN troops entered Los Angeles to restore order. Tomorrow they will be grateful. When presented with this scenario, individual rights will be willingly relinquished for the guarantee of their well-being granted to them by the World Government."*

The controllers know that individual freedoms will be surrendered for personal safety. *"Once the people are terrorised, you can force a police state on them,"* said journalist Mae Brussell.

It is true. Most people want an easy life. Fearing death, they willingly exchange their freedoms for the dangled carrot of peace and safety, oblivious to any nefarious activities unfolding around them.

Whatever manufactured crisis materialises next, be it virus, war, cyber attack or street riots, the conditioned masses will roll over every time, click their remote, sip their beer and fall sluggishly asleep till civilisation crumbles into oblivion.

Kindred Spirits in Opposition to Western Civilization

It is bizarre how certain ideologues side with Islam, when Islam is completely at odds with their worldview.

Nothing surprises in clown world, where ignorant blue haired Western protesters parade banners, 'Queers for Palestine'. Try being queer in Palestine, or some other parts of the Muslim world. Homosexuality is illegal in the Gaza Strip. In Saudi Arabia the punishment is death by stoning. Many will also recall the disturbing footage of Islamic state dropping gay men off buildings.

Hatred towards Christians for their faith in the Bible contrasts with overlooking extreme ideas held by many Muslims concealed in Islamic dogma.

No true follower of Christ would entertain killing a homosexual man. But in this cultural madness, radical Islam is increasingly normalised and accepted, and peace-loving Christians ostracised and hated.

In Western civilization, individuals have the autonomy to decide the course of their private lives. Freewill is a

Biblical value upon which western society was built. The fact that the good aspects of western nations were founded upon Christian principles cannot be escaped, no matter how much people want to deny it today.

Harbouring such vitriol for all that is true, these ideologues, whipped up by the establishment, conspire with common enemy groups.

Movements such as Extinction Rebellion, Just Stop Oil, Antifa, BLM, LGBTQ+, among others, are far from the genuine grassroots representation they claim to uphold. They serve as mere fronts for globalist kingpins like George Soros. His Open Society Foundation, who funds such organisations, shares objectives with the World Economic Forum, aiming for a de facto world government. These ideological advocates will go to the extent of utilising Islam in their quest to oppose truth. Anything to undermine the foundational elements of Western civilisation.

Nothing could have been clearer at the Women's March of 2017. 225,000 feminists converged on Washington wearing pink 'pussy power hats' representing women's rights.

The Pussyhat Project website explains, *'we unapologetically stand for women's rights.'* These advocators of women liberation walked alongside Muslim women wearing the hijab, a symbol of women's forced submission and men's hegemonic superiority.

This fusion of opposites was called upon by CAIR, the Council on American-Islamic Relation, who in 2009 was listed by the U.S. government as an unindicted co-conspirator in a scheme that provided funding to the terror group Hamas.

Fast forward just a few years later to 2023 and a shocking number of westerners fail to denounce Hamas as a terrorist group. The normalisation of Islamic extremism is upon us. This approval facilitates the globalist goal to replace Western civilisation. Islam is a mere pawn to be played in the globalist endgame.

The War Against Rationality

Casualties of the information war, these ideological social justice warriors, rabidly tear down everything that is good, right, and wholesome. All that positively builds a society must be destroyed. That is why traditional marriage and family is so vehemently under attack.

To silence those espousing traditional values, basic common sense and moral judgment, baseless slurs are repeatedly employed by the mainstream media, the institutions, and politicians in order to sway public opinion.

Today, individuals who embrace critical thinking are often subjected to ridicule, labelled bigots, far-right, white privilege, transphobic, anti-vaxxer, covidiot, Nazi, fascist, racist, nationalist, xenophobe, Putinphile, conspiracy theorist, religious fundamentalist, and the absurd list goes on, highlighting a disturbing backlash against those who simply question and analyse the establishment narrative.

An inversion of all that is good is afoot. Good is evil, evil is good. Ideology supplants morality. Evil is celebrated, ugly is glorified, beauty repulsed, body loathing and mutilation praised.

Much modern art and contemporary architecture is a

manifestation of this societal decadence. The art is ugly for a reason. It is used to further indoctrinate the individual, to subdue creativity, vanquish hope and extinguish personal ambition. It is the antithesis of all art before it.

We are taught to hate our nation, despise our heritage, loath our past and to pull down our history. We are forced into trading our national identity for superficial flags and political ideologies, ironically rooted in the very offenses that truth advocates are accused of.

In his novel 1984, of a dystopian future, George Orwell foresaw exactly what is taking place today —

"Every record has been destroyed or falsified, every book rewritten, every picture has been repainted, every statue and street building has been renamed, every date has been altered. And the process is continuing day by day and minute by minute. History has stopped. Nothing exists except an endless present in which the Party is always right".

Nothing happens by chance. This is a longstanding plot aimed at destroying Western society.

Today holiness is abhorred, while being unholy is feverishly celebrated. Sam Smith's song of the same title sensationally illustrates this societal decent into degeneracy. In Smith's purposeful shock music video, he impersonates Satan no less, with scantily clad females in cages writhing around the flames of hell. A porn star and drag queen are thrown in for good measure too. This mindless display, as Smith stares psychotically into the camera, while waggling his tongue about is ritualistically grooming young people into the system.

This is not happenstance, a fad, or the natural evolution of society, as those who suffer from reality denial would claim. No, there is a strategic and deliberate orchestrated war being waged against western civilisation.

Just four decades ago, television shows celebrated beautiful female vocalists, elegantly adorned in glamorous, long, glittering dresses, while serenading the audience with moving songs about love between a man and a woman.

Where have all the good women gone? Today, crass and near naked, they gyrate on stage like escapees from a mental institution. This kind of debauchery used to happen in some seedy back street theatre where shameful men letch in secret. Now it is public and open for all to see including the young.

Are the progressive parents shocked? Of course not. They are too busy at the local library watching their little children twerk along with bearded drag queens and encouraging them to stuff money down their frilly underwear. But I'm such a prude. After all, it is only a bit of innocent fun, I am told. So too, the normalisation of pedophilia gathers pace.

Everything is out in the open now. *"We're here, we're queer, we're coming for your children,"* cried the 2023 New York City annual Drag March. The chant echoing the theme of the San Francisco Gay Men's Chorus in 2021, who produced a music video promising to convert children to LGBTQ ideology.

The Gay Men's Chorus shamelessly sang —

"We'll convert your children, happens bit by bit,
quietly and subtly and you will barely notice it.
And you'll be disgusted when they start learning
things online
that you kept far from their sight.
We're coming for them.
We're coming for your children.
The gay agenda is coming home.
The gay agenda is here."

Furthermore, TEDx speaker, Mirjam Heine, argued that, *"pedophilia is a natural sexual orientation,"* Heine spoke at the University of Würtzberg in Germany, and said that pedophilia is like any other sexual orientation.

Yesterday's perverts are today's 'Minor-attracted persons', a phrase coined by the European Union as part of a campaign to recategorise child abusers as simply adults sexually attracted to children.

Today our world celebrates pride. Gone are the times of innocent carnival floats with fairy tale characters. Now, men in bondage gear simulate gay sex acts to cheering onlookers as they drive by.

What happened to common decency, being humble and kind-hearted? 'Be selfish', is today's mantra.

That was the good cheer message behind the 2023 Christmas commercial from the once respected high street chain Marks and Spencer. Not bearing to use 'Christ' and renaming the season 'Thismas', the advert went on a bizarre anarchic rampage, destroying timeless traditions that have brought families together for decades. But that is the point. Family must be destroyed so the people cannot unite and know true love. Orphaned, they become vassals to be cynically manipulated by the system in order to support and sustain the system.

This ideology, wars on the past. It reinvents society, denies biology, despises masculinity, loathes true femininity, glorifies homosexuality, celebrates transgenderism, compels speech, alters reality, abandons responsibility, and removes the requirement to live according to moral truth. Ideology trumps morality.

Humanity has been programmed to activate its own

extinction button. Civilisation now teeters on the brink of collapse. The false apocalyptic scenarios of the globalist regime employed to terrorise people into submission, pale into insignificance when faced with the reality of the real catastrophe ahead.

A Quest for the Solution in Troubled Times

Those awake, see what is imminently approaching. Like a startled rabbit caught in the headlights, they stare shocked at our world falling into tyranny. From every nation, language and creed, people trumpet the warning. They throng the cities, cry out in the streets, gather in parks, post relentlessly on social media, all in a desperate bid to wake up anyone who might stir from the dream state and listen.

But it is not in protests, people power, or any other goodly human endeavour that will halt the upending of civilisation and a Great Reset from dawning upon humanity.

Recognising the existence of evil is the first step towards prevailing in the struggle against the darkness sweeping the planet.

The war against people transcends the physical realm, it is a confrontation with evil itself, demanding a spiritual response.

According to biblical teachings, Satan is the ruler of this world, blinding unbelievers so they cannot know the truth. The Bible also refers to Satan as the prince of the power of the air, thus influencing the mainstream media. Cast out of heaven to earth along with his angels, he deceives the whole world. Called the Father of Lies, this malevolent spiritual entity is in direct conflict with humanity, embodying those identified as the sons of disobedience to enact his endgame.

Armed with this knowledge we understand that all human effort and natural resistance is futile against a supernatural force of wickedness.

Humanity urgently needs a formidable saviour, one capable of defeating the relentless forces of darkness, determined to cull and enslave humanity forever.

Does a saviour exist, and if yes, who might it be?

Over 2000 years ago a man came into the world. Ancient writings record his arrival —

'The people living in darkness have seen a great light; on those living in the land of the shadow of death, a light has dawned'.

He is the man society has been conditioned to reject as a fable in favour of evolutionary theory. Eliminating God is a strategy of the controllers who declare themselves to be all powerful.

Yuval Noah Harari, advisor to the World Economic Forum declared, *'We are in the process of becoming gods and the big question that faces us is what to do with our new god-like powers.'* Harari was commenting on the impact of artificial intelligence and bioengineering upon the human race. For instance, Elon Musk's Neuralink, brain implant, officially received FDA approval for human clinical trials in May 2023, dovetailing with WEF Chairman, Klaus Schwab's chip in the head prediction by 2026. In the near future it will be possible to control computers, smartphones, televisions, smart home devices, smart vehicles, make payments and more, with the mind.

Amidst cries of conspiracy, those sincerely seeking insights into the future of our world should study the realm of human augmentation. The aforementioned Ministry of Defence document, available for download on the British Government website, delves into this subject, encompassing elements such as DNA editing and vaccines as components of their upgrade strategy.

But should the globalists succeed in humanity's upgrade, people will still be a far cry from divinity.

The man who came into our world to save it, was the one denigrated outside Jerusalem, Israel, over two millennia ago. Still mocked today, his name used as a common curse word.

Historical writings said, the reason this man appeared was to destroy Satan's work. He also declared his supremacy over Satan.

But so too society has been conditioned to reject this personification of evil that afflicts the world. Science has relegated this spiritual entity to a primitive past. If Satan is a fable too, the question must be asked, from where does evil originate? Many deny its existence, even in the face of mounting evidence. But is it honestly believable that heinous acts can be committed in the absence of evil?

If the prevailing belief suggests intrinsic human goodness, why does our world seem to darken with each passing hour? To comprehend this, one must acknowledge the contrary notion: a predisposition towards evil exists within people.

The saviour of the world was born over 2000 years ago. His name is Jesus. Of himself he said, *"the reason I came was to testify to the truth, and all those on the side of truth listen to my voice."*

The question must be asked. Are we on the side of truth today? Can we hear the voice of Jesus Christ? Or do we hear the opinions of the mainstream media and our own unbelieving heart?

For those seeking deliverance from the prevailing darkness in our world, the solution lies in embracing the light. Christ proclaimed, *"I am the light of the world. If you follow me, you won't have to walk in darkness, for you will have the light that leads to life."*

It is crucial not to conflate Christ with institutionalised religion. Organised Christianity lacks the power to rescue us from the world's horrors; instead, it often imposes control and bondage. True salvation is found not in ceremonies and rituals but in cultivating a dynamic relationship with God through Christ Jesus.

In a powerful reminder, Christ extends an invitation: *"Look! I stand at the door and knock. If you hear my voice and open the door, I will come in, and we will share a meal together as friends."* (Revelation 3:20).

As our world descends further into darkness—marked by cultural confusion, escalating violence, and the erosion of democratic values, as Western democracies morph into tyrannical dictatorships, as virus, war and terrorism rock the nations, and The Great Reset descends upon humanity —those who follow Christ remain unshaken. They are not subject to the prevailing darkness but are guided by God's light.

By embracing Christ, we experience liberation from the primary tool wielded by the globalists — the fear of death, rendering us immune to control or coercion. Christ offers freedom from conformity to The Great Reset and delivers us from Satan, the god of this world.

For those who see this world as hellish, a greater hell awaits followers of the globalists and the devil. Christ stands as the ultimate Saviour, poised to end The Great Reset and dispense justice to the wicked.

It is time to explore the Bible; perhaps there's one within your home. Delve into the gospel of John, learn about Jesus' life and how we should live ours. Also unveil startling prophecies that anticipated everything detailed in *The Great Delusion* — the establishment of a one-world government, a cashless society, and the requirement for a distinct mark during transactions — be it a chip or QR code tattoo.

The Scriptures also predict deception through pharmaceuticals, a reality evident today, as well as the global deception orchestrated by Satan through a reality-blinding medium like television.

Christ's predictions of deadly pestilence and wars, now unfolding on an unprecedented scale, affirm the truth and reliability of the Bible. In light of this, when Jesus declared, *"I am the truth," "My peace I give to you"*, and *"I will be with you until the end,"* in confident trust we can believe it, no matter what calamity comes upon this troubled world.

In these trying times, the call to turn to the Light of the world resonates more than ever. Time is of the essence, and none of us knows how much we have left.

In humble reverence, let us open our hearts and direct our spirits towards our Creator, embracing the redemptive grace offered through His Son, Jesus Christ.

With contrition, let us earnestly seek God's forgiveness, acknowledging our role in a world that refuses to acknowledge Him. Imploring His divine mercy, may we be liberated from the entanglements of our sin and delivered from the prevailing wickedness of this era, allowing us to live free in Christ's transforming light.

So what are we waiting for?

To thoroughly explore the themes discussed in *The Great Delusion,* a surface Google search will prove inadequate. Stories disproving mainstream narratives are routinely hidden from search results. In a landscape marked by restricted speech, cursory inquiries will result in encounters with fact-checking websites that dismiss the content presented in this book. Uncovering the truth necessitates a thorough and time consuming process.

Furthermore, as a starting point, consider also turning to uncensored platforms that champion free speech, such as *BitChute* or *Rumble.*

Every success in your quest to unravel the truth and gain firsthand insights into the realities shaping our world.

Other books by Jason Carter

Trumpet Blast Warning
Unabridged Edition

After experiencing a dramatic wake up call Jason Carter began a period of intensive research about the connection between end-time Bible prophecies and contemporary events on the world stage.

In Trumpet Blast Warning you will discover how;

• Minds are being manipulated through mass media propaganda

• Freedoms and democracy are being subtly eroded

• National sovereignties are being replaced by a one world government

• Human catastrophes are not always as 'accidental' as they seem

• Technology and surveillance are being used to control and oppress

• The anti-Christ spirit is intensifying all over the earth

• The world is gearing up for the climactic events of history

Unless the trumpet is sounded no one will get ready. Jason Carter's book sounds an unequivocal trumpet blast warning and rallies everyone to be prepared.

Available on Amazon, paperback and Kindle.

Beyond Earthly Realms

In this companion volume to his acclaimed *Trumpet Blast Warning*, Jason Carter gives us heaven's perspective on earth's future. Prepare to be challenged.

Whether you are a believer or not the revelations in this book will not leave you unmoved.

It truly is time to get ready.

Available on Amazon, paperback and Kindle.

Trumpet Blast Warning
Concise and Updated Edition

The Concise and Updated Edition of *Trumpet Blast Warning* includes the latest on fake news, world government, creating a climate of fear, government sponsored terrorism, advancement of the European Union superstate, the rise of Islam, occult practices of politicians, one world religion, cashless society, surveillance, world war three, and the migrant crisis.

Available on Amazon, paperback and Kindle.

Visit the authors website

www.endtimehour.co.uk

Printed in Great Britain
by Amazon